Karen B. Turnage

PO Box 74844

Richmond, VA 23236

www.abundantlivingpublishing.com

BROKEN BUT NOT SHATTERED

by Karen B. Turnage

The Journey & Strength of Overcoming Relationship & Financial Brokenness

Cover design by Karen B. Turnage

Editing by Karen B. Turnage

ABUNDANT LIVING
PUBLISHING
JOHN 10:10

Published by
Karen B. Turnage of Abundant Living Publishing

Author: Karen B. Turnage

ISBN: 979-8-234-17180-1

Printed in the United States of America

Contents

Broken But Not Shattered

by Karen B. Turnage

Forward by Bishop Daniel Robertson, Jr., Senior Pastor of Mt. Gilead Full Gospel International Ministries Chesterfield, Virginia

*"And they overcame him by the blood of the Lamb, and by the word of their **testimony**; and they loved not their lives unto the death." **Revelation 12:11. KJV***

So often, we hear great testimonies related to the great things GOD has done. Many get fascinated by the end result but skip over the middle journey. The testimonies of results are good and have the ability to bring hope. However, few people are willing to open-up their lives to share their mistakes, blunders, and what they learned from them.

In this book**,** Karen Turnage uses her personal life to teach you life lessons! Different people learn things through different methods. One way is hearing someone else's personal journey. What you are being introduced to is basically a biography. As you read the following pages, it will be hard not to learn, because of the way things will be spelled out to you.

I'm excited for you, the reader, because you are about to see how you too can recover from mistakes. We all make mistakes and Satan uses these mistakes to convince us that there is no recovery. As you read, you will be encouraged to ***get-up*** from bad decisions. Karen shares her personal testimony transparently with the reader in hopes that you will walk away believing you too have the ability to come back from your mistakes, blunders, rejection, financial debt, whatever it might be ... knowing - ***"there is always a way you can recover".***

It is my prayer that reading her testimony will awaken your spirit, light a fire within you, and inspire you to keep fighting for your victory.

Finally, I often preach *"you are not defeated until you quit, so my advice to you -* ***don't quit****!*

Forward by My Loving Daughter, Sheniqua Jackson

I would first like to tell you how incredibly proud I am of you. Not only for writing this book, but for overcoming every obstacle that has been thrown your way since birth. You have always taken your struggles and found a way to keep them from defining you or holding you back.

You prayed to have a daughter, and that is exactly what God gave you—the desire of your heart. You prepared for me before I was even born, which reflects something you have done throughout your entire life: **you continuously position and prepare yourself for greatness.**

Now, back to me—LOL!

Because of the way you were raised and the things you experienced, you were grateful for what you had, but you wanted something better for me. You made sure I was loved and cared for—not only through your words, but through your actions.

You have always taught me that **love is an action word**, and you have lived that before me.

You worked hard to give me the best childhood you could, even during times when I didn't understand the struggles you were experiencing behind the scenes. As a little girl, I didn't know about the financial pressures, sacrifices, or worries. I simply knew that my mother loved me. I especially remember our Fridays. You would pick me up from daycare, and I got to choose where we would eat that day. Something that may have seemed so simple became a special memory between us. We have so many memories together—and, of course, you will never let me forget any of them!

As you began developing your relationship with God, you took me along on that journey with you. Eventually, I realized that this was exactly where we needed to be.

I remember writing on a sticky note:

"God will make a way for you and me."

And He has not failed us yet.

Thank you for being the best mother you knew how to be and for inspiring me to become the best version of myself. You have poured—and continue to pour—so much wisdom into me as I navigate this thing called life.

This book is only the beginning. I believe it is one of many books to come and is simply setting the tone for everything God has placed inside of you.

Broken...But Not Shattered is a book for everyone, but I especially believe it is for the woman who feels as though **life has been "lifing" a little too hard**—the woman who has endured so much that she wonders if her breakthrough will ever come.

To that woman, I want to say:

God has not forgotten about you.

Keep going. Keep pushing. Keep praying. You are not alone.

You may have been broken by some of the things you have experienced, but you do not have to remain shattered. You can overcome. You can heal. You can rise. And you can still become the woman God ordained you to be.

Mom, your life is proof of that.

Your struggles didn't destroy you. Your hardships didn't stop you. The pressure didn't break you beyond repair. Instead, God used it all to develop the woman you are today.

Diamonds are formed under pressure—and now it is your time to shine brightly.

I am proud to call you my mother, and I am even more excited for the world to experience your story.

I love you, Mom.

Your Daughter,

Sheniqua Jackson

Broken But Not Shattered

by Karen B. Turnage

ACKNOWLEDGEMENTS

To God Be the Glory

To God be all the glory—the Author and Finisher of my life.

Lord, you have been so good to me, even during the times when I wasn't good to myself. I thank You for every trial, every tribulation, every joy, and every disappointment, because I now understand that they were all necessary to prepare me for my destiny and purpose.

I dedicate this book to You because it was You who placed the desire in my heart to share the gifts You have entrusted to me with Your people. Every page of this book is a testimony of Your faithfulness, grace, mercy, and unfailing love.

Without You, there would be no story to tell.

Without You, there would be no healing.

Without You, there would be no restoration.

Without You, there would be no *Broken...But Not Shattered.*

For every blessing, every breakthrough, every lesson, and every victory, I simply say...**Thank You**

To My Spiritual Parents

To my Pastor, ***Bishop Daniel Robertson, Jr.***, and ***Co-Pastor Elena Robertson***, my spiritual father and mother—

Thank you both for the countless years of pouring into my life through your teaching, wisdom, prayers, and unwavering example. Your impartation has helped shape not only my spiritual walk but also the woman I continue to become.

You have consistently modeled excellence, integrity, servant leadership, and what it truly means to live a Kingdom-centered life. Because of your example, I strive to walk in excellence and reflect the principles you have faithfully taught.

Thank you for believing in me, encouraging my gifts, and giving me the opportunity of a lifetime to serve alongside you in advancing the Kingdom of God. Your investment in my life will forever be appreciated, and I pray that I continue to make you proud.

To My Loving Husband

To my dear husband, **James C. Turnage, III**

Thank you for standing beside me through every season of life.

Thank you for your unwavering love, your patience, your

encouragement, and your tireless support of every dream, vision, and endeavor God has placed in my heart. You have always allowed me the freedom to walk boldly in my gifts without complaint, and that has meant more to me than words can adequately express.

Thank you for believing in me, praying for me, celebrating my victories, and loving me through every challenge.

Your love has been a gift from God, and I am grateful that He brought our lives back together according to His perfect timing.

I love you, appreciate you, and thank God for you every day.

To My Precious Daughter

To my wonderful daughter, **Sheniqua** —

You have always been, and will always be, Mommy's Baby Girl.

Thank you for allowing me the joy and privilege of loving you with all my heart. Watching you grow into the beautiful woman you are today has been one of the greatest blessings of my life.

It is my prayer that this book becomes a source of encouragement, wisdom, and strength for you in the years ahead. May it remind you that no matter what life brings, God is always faithful, and with Him, nothing is impossible.

I look forward to continuing to make beautiful memories together as we grow, laugh, learn, and experience all that God has planned for our lives. Never forget how deeply you are loved—not only by me, but by God. I love you more than words can express.

In Loving Memory of My Daddy

In loving memory of my Daddy, **Thomas Ervin Blowe**, affectionately known as **"Blowe."**

Daddy, you were more than my father—you were my best friend, my confidant, my protector, and one of my greatest supporters. There isn't a day that goes by that I don't think about you or miss your presence in my life.

I hope that I have made you proud. I wish you were still here so I could share with you all the incredible things God has done—and continues to do—in my life. I would love nothing more than to tell you about His faithfulness, His grace, and how He has fulfilled promises that once seemed impossible.

This book is a testament to God's restoring power, and I know you would have celebrated every page with me. I can almost hear your words of encouragement and see that proud smile on your face.

Although I miss you deeply, I find comfort in knowing that you are resting peacefully in the presence of the Lord. Your love, wisdom, and the memories we shared will forever remain in my heart.

Thank you for believing in me, loving me unconditionally, and being such an important part of my life's journey. Until we meet again, Daddy...I love you, I miss you, and I will carry your memory with me always.

> **May you continue to rest peacefully in the arms of our Lord and Savior, Jesus Christ.**

To My Mother

Thank you for choosing life for me at the tender age of sixteen. I will always be grateful for your courage and the sacrifice you made to bring me into this world.

Before I even understood the importance of self-care, you were teaching me its value through your actions. You took pride in caring for my hair, my nails, my hygiene, and the way I dressed. You made sure I always presented my best outward appearance, and those early lessons have remained with me throughout my life.

Thank you for giving me my first example of self-care and personal dignity. Although our journey was not without challenges, I will always cherish the care you poured into me during those formative years. Your decision to choose life gave me the opportunity to fulfill God's purpose for my life, and for that, I am forever thankful.

To My Stepmother

In loving memory of my Stepmother, Rebecca Blowe, aka "Sue" Thank you for caring for me during my adolescent years. Your guidance and nurturing helped shape me into the young lady I was becoming.

Thank you for teaching me life skills that have stayed with me throughout the years—from cooking and caring for a home to the importance of hospitality. You showed me how to welcome guests with warmth, create joyful memories, and embrace life's special moments with laughter and love.

Your influence extended far beyond the practical lessons you taught. You helped instill confidence, grace, and an appreciation for family, fellowship, and enjoying the blessings of life. I will always be grateful for the role you played in my journey and for the love and care you shared with me.

Though you are no longer here, your legacy lives on in the values you passed down. You will always hold a special place in my heart, and your memory will forever be cherished.

To My Grandmother

I honor the loving memory of my grandmother, **Mable**

Brice, affectionately known as **"Nanny."**

Thank you for caring for me as a little girl and for teaching me manners, respect, and values that I still carry with me today. The lessons you taught me have become a lasting part of who I am.

Thank you for the delicious Sunday dinners that brought our family together around the table with love. Those meals nourished more than our bodies—they nourished our hearts and created memories that I will cherish forever.

And thank you for faithfully sending me those "Little Girl" birthday cards every year, even after I had become an adult. That simple tradition always reminded me that, in your eyes, I would forever be your little granddaughter. It was one of the many ways you showed your unconditional love.

May you continue to rest peacefully in the presence of the Lord. I like to imagine you in Heaven doing what you loved so much—cooking, baking, and blessing everyone around you with your love. Your legacy lives on in our family, and your memory will forever hold a special place in my heart.

With all my love, until we meet again.

To My Family

To all of my family, please know that I love each and every

one of you and truly want God's very best for your lives. Each of you has touched my life in your own unique way, and for that, I am deeply grateful. Thank you for the love, the memories, the lessons, and even the challenges that have all helped shape the woman I am today A special thank you to my aunts, **"Honey" and "Doll,"** for being wonderful examples during my childhood. I admired your education, professional careers, and the lives you created for yourselves. Honey, I even tried teaching myself shorthand because I wanted to be like you! I also admired you and Jan for traveling and hoped that one day I would be able to do the same. I thank God for each of you, and I pray His continued blessings upon your lives.

My Lifelong Best Friend

To my lifelong best friend, **Kimberly Bell**—

Girl, words could never fully express how grateful I am for our friendship of more than 45 years! We have shared so many unforgettable moments, countless conversations about life, and more laughter than I can count. Through every season, you've been a constant source of love, encouragement, and friendship.

Thank you for standing by my side through the highs and the lows. Here's to many more years of making memories, sharing laughs, and enjoying this journey together. And yes, let's keep laughing together—even when we don't have any teeth! I love you, my friend.

DEDICATIONS

This book is lovingly dedicated to my husband, **James C. Turnage, III**, for your unwavering love, encouragement, and steadfast support. Thank you for loving me through it all. I love you so much Babe!

To the loving memory of my Daddy, **Thomas Ervin Blowe ("Blowe")**, thank you for believing in me and helping shape the woman I have become. Your love and legacy will forever live in my heart.

To my precious daughter, **Sheniqua**, you will always be Mommy's Baby Girl. May this book inspire you to trust God through every season of life and always remember that no matter how broken life may seem, God can restore all things.

This book is dedicated to everyone who has ever felt broken, rejected, forgotten, or overlooked. May my testimony remind you that God is still in the business of restoring lives. You may be broken...but by His grace, you never have to remain shattered.

I love you all—yesterday, today, and always.

Broken But Not Shattered

by Karen B. Turnage

PREFACE

Life has a way of breaking us.

Sometimes the brokenness comes through rejection. Sometimes it comes through poor decisions, financial hardship, failed relationships, disappointment, loss, or the weight of circumstances beyond our control. Whatever the source, brokenness can leave us questioning our worth, our purpose, and even God's plan for our lives.

For many years, I carried wounds that no one could see. Behind my smile were moments of pain, uncertainty, and struggles. I experienced rejection, searched for love in the wrong places, battled financial challenges, and faced seasons when I wondered if life would ever be different.

Yet through every trial, one truth remained constant: **God never left me.**

This book is not about portraying a perfect life. It is about sharing an honest one.

Broken But Not Shattered is my testimony of God's redeeming love, restoring grace, and unfailing faithfulness. Every chapter reflects a season of my journey—from childhood experiences that shaped my identity to financial setbacks, broken relationships, personal growth, and ultimately discovering the abundant life that God had planned for me all along.

As you read these pages, my prayer is that you will see yourself somewhere in my story. Perhaps you've experienced rejection. Perhaps you've struggled financially, questioned your purpose, or wondered whether God could ever use someone with your past. If so, I want you to know that you are not alone.

One of the greatest lessons I have learned is that God does not waste our pain. He uses every experience—both the joyful and the painful—to prepare us for His purpose. What once seemed like the greatest obstacles in my life became the very foundation of my testimony.

This book is not simply about surviving brokenness; it is about discovering that brokenness is often the beginning of God's restoration. It is about learning that our scars can become symbols of His grace, our struggles can become someone else's encouragement, and our testimony can become a beacon of hope for those who are still searching for healing.

My desire is that when you reach the final page, you will walk away with renewed faith, fresh hope, and the confidence to believe that no matter what has happened in your life, God is still writing your story.

If He could restore me, He can restore you.

Thank you for allowing me the privilege of sharing my heart, my journey, and the lessons God has faithfully taught me along the way. It is my prayer that these pages encourage you to trust God completely, embrace His process, and never lose sight of the purpose He has placed within you.

Always remember...You may be broken.

But through God's grace, His love, and His restoring power...

You never have to be shattered.

To God be all the glory.

Karen B. Turnage, Author

Broken But Not Shattered

Broken But Not Shattered

by Karen B. Turnage

ABOUT THE AUTHOR

Karen B. Turnage is an author, financial coach, entrepreneur, and passionate advocate for helping others discover healing, purpose, financial freedom, and abundant living through Christ.

Karen's story began in **Goochland County, Virginia**, where she spent the first ten years of her childhood living without many of the conveniences that others may have taken for granted. Her childhood home had no running water, indoor plumbing, or central heating. She learned early what it meant to work with what you had—pumping water from a well and helping cut wood to provide heat for the home.

At the age of ten, Karen's life changed significantly when she moved to the West End of Richmond to live with her father and stepmother. That transition became part of a much larger journey marked by childhood rejection, blended-family challenges, broken relationships, financial hardship, personal adversity, and ultimately, restoration. Rather than allowing those experiences to define her, Karen came to recognize that many of the painful chapters of her life were preparing her for purpose.

Having personally experienced the burden of debt and financial instability, Karen developed a passion for helping others achieve financial freedom. As the founder of **Abundant Living Community Services**, she is committed to empowering individuals and families through financial coaching, life-skills education, practical financial strategies, and encouragement. Her desire is to help people become whole—**spiritually, emotionally, and financially**.

Karen also serves faithfully in ministry and has used her God-given gifts in numerous areas throughout her life. She enjoys encouraging, teaching, mentoring, creating, and helping others recognize the possibilities within themselves.

Her first book, ***Broken But Not Shattered: The Journey and Strength of Overcoming Relationship & Financial Brokenness,*** is a transparent testimony of God's faithfulness throughout her life. Through personal experiences, biblical principles, and lessons learned through both successes and mistakes, Karen reminds readers that being broken does not mean being destroyed. With God, the broken pieces of our lives can become part of something greater than we ever imagined.

Karen resides in Virginia with her husband, **James C. Turnage, III**, and treasures her roles as a wife, mother, author, entrepreneur, and lifelong learner. Her greatest desire is that her testimony will encourage others to believe that regardless of where they started, what they have endured, or how many times life has knocked them down, **God still has a purpose for their lives.**

Her favorite reminder summarizes her journey in three simple words:

"Nobody But God!"

Because when Karen looks back at where she started, considers everything she survived, and sees where God has brought her today, there is simply no other explanation.

"Your brokenness is not the end of your story—it may simply be the beginning of God's greatest work in your life."
— Karen B. Turnage

Broken But Not Shattered

by Karen B. Turnage

INTRODUCTION

Have you ever wondered why certain things happened in your life?

Have you ever questioned why God allowed the heartbreak, the rejection, the financial struggles, or the painful seasons that seemed to have no purpose?

I certainly have.

There were times when I asked God, **"Why me?"** There were moments when I believed my past would define my future and that the mistakes I had made would forever disqualify me from living the life God intended for me. Like many people, I searched for love, acceptance, security, and validation in places that could never truly satisfy the longing in my heart.

But God...Those two words changed everything.

What I once viewed as broken pieces of my life, God was carefully using to build a beautiful testimony. Every disappointment, every setback, every tear, every financial struggle, every broken relationship, and every painful lesson became part of His divine plan. Looking back now, I realize that nothing was wasted.

Broken But Not Shattered is more than my story—it is a

testimony of God's faithfulness. Within these pages, I invite you to walk alongside me as I share some of the most vulnerable moments of my life. From childhood rejection and searching for love, to financial brokenness and discovering my God-given purpose, I pray my journey will remind you that God specializes in restoration. He is able to take what appears to be broken beyond repair and transform it into something beautiful for His glory.

This book is not written because I have lived a perfect life. It is written because I serve a perfect God who never abandoned me, even when I wandered away from Him. His grace covered me, His mercy sustained me, and His love continually called me back to His purpose.

If you have ever felt rejected...
If you have ever struggled financially...
If you have ever questioned your worth...
If you have ever wondered whether God could still use someone with your past...

This book is for you.

My hope is that as you read these chapters, you will not simply see my story—you will begin to recognize your own. Perhaps your circumstances are different, but the same God who restored my life is able to restore yours.

As you journey through this book, I encourage you to be honest with yourself. Allow God to reveal areas where healing is needed. Reflect on the lessons at the end of each chapter. Pray the prayers. Answer the reflection questions. Most importantly, trust God's process, even when you cannot understand His purpose.

I have learned that brokenness is not the end of the story.

Sometimes, it is where God begins His greatest work.

Today, I stand as living proof that your past does not determine your future, your failures do not define your identity, and your brokenness does not disqualify you from God's promises.

No matter what you've experienced, there is hope.

There is healing.

There is restoration.

There is purpose.

And there is abundant life through Jesus Christ.

As you turn these pages, I pray you will be encouraged to release your pain, embrace God's purpose, and believe that what feels like the end may actually be the beginning of the greatest chapter of your life.

Welcome to my journey.

More importantly, welcome to the beginning of your own healing. Because with God...**You may be broken...But you never have to be shattered.**

Karen B. Turnage, *Author,*

Broken But Not Shattered

Chapter 1
Childhood Rejection
"Broken, But Never Beyond God's Reach"

> ***"Though my father and mother forsake me, then the Lord will take me up."***
>
> ***—Psalm 27:10 (KJV)***

There are moments in life that shape who we become long before we understand why they happened. Some people are born into homes overflowing with affection, security, and stability. Others begin life carrying questions they never asked for and wounds they never chose.

I was one of those children.

Every story has a beginning, and mine began with a young mother who gave birth to me on *her* sixteenth birthday.

Yes, we share the same birthday. She was still a child herself, trying to navigate the challenges of adolescence while carrying the responsibility of bringing me into the world. Looking back through the eyes of an adult, I realize she did the very best she could with the knowledge, strength, and resources she had at the time. She made sure my hair was neatly done, my nails were cared for, and I was dressed well. She taught me the importance of taking pride in my appearance long before I understood the meaning of self-care. While my mother worked to provide for me, my grandmother lovingly became my primary caregiver, giving me the nurturing and stability every child needs. Eventually, when my mother could no longer provide for me financially, she made the difficult decision to allow my father and stepmother to raise me. At the time, I couldn't understand why my life was changing, but years later I realized that each person who helped raise me was part of God's divine plan. What felt like rejection in my childhood would ultimately become the foundation for the testimony God was writing through my life.

Before I was old enough to understand words like *rejection*, *abandonment*, or *blended family*, I was already living them.

My story began with a decision that changed the course of my life forever. As a child, I couldn't comprehend the circumstances surrounding that decision. I only knew that I wasn't being raised by the woman who had given birth to me.

For years, I wrestled with silent questions.

Why wasn't I enough?

Why wasn't I wanted?

What was wrong with me?

Those questions echoed through my childhood, even when no one else could hear them.

A Family That Didn't Look Like Mine

Life became even more complicated because my stepmother had very little opportunity to know me before I came into her life at the age of 10. In many ways, we were strangers trying to become family overnight.

To make matters more unusual, my biological mother and my stepmother were pregnant at nearly the same time. My brother and I are only one month apart in age.

As children, we grew up side by side.

Yet even though we shared a home, I often wondered where I truly belonged.

Blended families can be beautiful, but they can also be complicated. Children often carry emotional burdens they don't have the words to explain. They notice differences. They recognize favoritism—even when adults believe they are hiding it.

Sometimes rejection isn't spoken.

Sometimes it's felt.

It can be found in the silence.

In the comparisons.

In the absence of affection.

In wondering if you really belong.

Those feelings quietly become part of your identity if they are never healed.

Becoming the Quiet Girl

As I grew older, my personality reflected the hurt I carried.

I became timid and shy.

Reserved.

I rarely believed my voice mattered.

Rather than drawing attention to myself, I learned to disappear into the background and be quiet.

People often assume quiet children have nothing to say.

The truth is, many quiet children have too much to say but no one they trust enough to tell.

I spent years hiding behind my smile.

I learned how to survive.

But surviving is different from living.

Every disappointment reinforced the lie that I wasn't enough.

Every rejection seemed to confirm what I secretly feared.

“If my own mother gave me away, maybe I’m not worth choosing.”

The enemy has a way of planting lies early.

The enemy knows that if he can convince a child they are unwanted or that their life was a mistake, he can keep them trapped in a lifelong pursuit of acceptance, approval, and validation from people—never realizing that they were already chosen, loved, and accepted by God. For many years, that’s exactly what I did.

The Weight of Comparison

Comparison is a heavy burden.

When another child seems to receive what you long for, it’s easy to wonder why your life feels different.

Comparison steals joy.

Comparison breeds insecurity.

Comparison whispers that someone else is more deserving.

Looking back now, I realize God never intended for me to compare my story to anyone else’s.

My journey was unique because my purpose was unique.

God wasn’t punishing me.

He was preparing me.

Although I couldn't see His hand then, He was already writing a story that would one day encourage countless others.

God Was There All Along

One of the greatest revelations I've received as an adult is realizing that God never abandoned me—even when I felt abandoned by people.

While I questioned my worth, He was calling me His daughter.

While I wondered if I belonged, Heaven had already prepared a place for me.

While I struggled with rejection, God was developing resilience.

He saw purpose where I only saw pain.

He saw a future financial coach while I struggled with insecurity.

He saw a business owner while I wondered if I mattered.

He saw an Author, Playwright, a Realtor, a Financial Accountant/Coach, an Administrator, a Graphic Designer and a successful Group Home Provider before I ever believed in myself.

The broken little girl had no idea that God would one day use every painful chapter of her life to become someone else's hope.

Pain became preparation.

Rejection became redirection.

Brokenness became the birthplace of purpose.

My Identity Was Never My Circumstances

Children often believe that what happens to them defines them.

Adults know differently.

Today I understand that my identity was never determined by who raised me.

It wasn't determined by who accepted me.

It wasn't determined by who rejected me.

My identity was established by God before I ever entered this world.

I am fearfully and wonderfully made.

I am chosen.

I am loved.

I am accepted.

I am enough.

Those truths took years to believe, but they eventually replaced every lie I had accepted during childhood.

Looking Back with Grace

Today, I don't tell this story to assign blame.

I tell it because healing begins when we stop pretending we were never hurt.

Forgiveness doesn't erase what happened.

It releases its power over your future.

As I matured spiritually, God taught me that everyone in my story was human.

People make decisions while carrying their own pain.

Sometimes broken people unintentionally break others.

That realization gave me compassion.

Instead of living as a victim, I chose to become a victor.

Instead of allowing rejection to define me, I allowed God to refine me.

The little girl who once questioned her worth would one day stand confidently, helping others rebuild their finances, discover their purpose, and believe that restoration is possible.

Only God could write a story like that.

Life Lessons

- *Your beginning does not determine your ending.*
- *Rejection is painful, but it is not permanent.*

- *Your identity comes from God, not people's opinions.*
- *Healing begins when honesty replaces denial.*
- *Forgiveness frees you to embrace God's future.*
- *God can use every painful experience for His glory.*

Reflection Questions

1. Have you ever believed a lie about yourself because of something that happened in childhood?
2. What areas of your life still need healing?
3. How has God protected you in ways you didn't recognize at the time?
4. What truth from God's Word can replace the lies you've believed?
5. Who do you need to forgive so you can move forward?

Chapter Prayer

Heavenly Father,

Thank You for loving me before I ever understood what love truly was. Thank You for seeing me when I felt invisible and choosing me when I felt rejected.

Today I surrender every childhood wound, every painful memory, and every lie that has tried to shape my identity. Heal the places in my heart that still ache. Replace rejection with acceptance, fear with confidence, loneliness with Your presence, and insecurity with the assurance that I am Your beloved child.

Teach me to forgive those who hurt me, whether intentionally or unintentionally. Help me release resentment so that I can walk freely into the purpose You created for me.

Thank You for proving that my past does not dictate my future. Thank You for taking broken pieces and creating something beautiful for Your glory.

May my story become a testimony that encourages others to trust You, even when life doesn't make sense.

I declare that I am no longer defined by rejection—I am defined by redemption.

In Jesus' name,

Amen.

Chapter 2

Teenaged Shenanigans

Looking for Acceptance in All the Wrong Places

"Train up a child in the way he should go: and when he is old, he will not depart from it."
—Proverbs 22:6 (KJV)

Teenage years are often described as the best years of life. For many, they are filled with excitement, friendships, and discovering who they are. For me, they became years of searching—searching for acceptance, identity, and a place where I truly belonged.

The brokenness I carried from childhood didn't simply disappear as I grew older. It followed me into my teenage years, quietly influencing my decisions, my friendships, and the way I viewed myself.

I wanted to be accepted.

I wanted to fit in.

I wanted someone to see my value.

Like many teenagers, I found myself standing at crossroads. One path led toward God's purpose, while the other promised temporary acceptance. At thirteen years old, I wasn't mature enough to understand that every decision would shape the woman I would eventually become.

A World of New Influences

At the age of thirteen, I was introduced to things that no young teenager should have been experimenting with.

Cigarettes.

Marijuana.

Alcohol.

Parties.

At first, it seemed harmless.

Everyone around me made it look normal.

The laughter was contagious.

The music was loud.

The atmosphere felt exciting.

For a little while, it seemed as if all my insecurities disappeared.

But deep inside, there was another voice.

A quiet voice.

A gentle voice.

A voice that reminded me that this wasn't who I was created to be.

Even before I fully understood God, I believe He was already speaking to my heart.

Every time I participated in something I knew wasn't right, there was an uneasiness I couldn't ignore.

I could smile on the outside while feeling convicted on the inside.

Trying to Fill an Empty Place

Looking back now, I realize I wasn't really looking for cigarettes, marijuana or parties.

I was looking for peace.

I was searching for acceptance.

I wasn't trying to rebel against God.

I was trying to escape the pain I hadn't learned how to process.

Many people judge outward behavior without understanding the inward wounds.

What looks like rebellion is often unresolved hurt.

What appears to be disobedience is sometimes a desperate cry to belong.

My heart wasn't evil.

It was hurting.

And hurting people often make unhealthy decisions while trying to heal themselves.

My First Love

During those early teenage years, something else happened that would leave a lasting impression on my life.

I met a young man who would later become my husband.

Neither of us could have imagined what God had planned.

At thirteen years old, we were simply two teenagers meeting during a season when life seemed full of possibilities.

There was no way I could have known that after years of life, heartbreak, growth, and separate journeys, God would eventually bring us back together.

Sometimes God allows people to enter our lives long before we understand their purpose.

His timing is always greater than ours.

The Battle Within

Even though I was making choices that didn't honor God, my conscience never became comfortable with them.

I knew right from wrong.

Every party ended.

Every high faded.

Every drink wore off.

But the emptiness always returned.

Nothing I tried could fill the place in my heart that belonged to God.

There is a difference between happiness and peace.
Happiness depends on circumstances.

Peace comes from God's presence.

I was chasing happiness while my soul longed for peace.

The Pressure to Belong

Teenagers often feel an overwhelming need to fit in.

Nobody wants to feel left out.

Nobody wants to be different.

I was no exception.

Sometimes the greatest temptation isn't the activity itself.

It's the fear of rejection if you say no.

Peer pressure doesn't always sound like someone forcing you to do something.

Sometimes it sounds like:

"Everybody's doing it."

"Don't be so uptight."

"Just this once."

"What's the big deal?"

Those words have influenced countless young lives.

I wish every teenager understood that fitting in is never worth losing yourself.

The crowd may applaud your choices today, but they won't always be there to help you recover from the consequences tomorrow.

God's Quiet Pursuit

One of the most beautiful truths I've discovered is that God never stopped pursuing me—even when I wasn't pursuing Him.

He didn't abandon me because I made mistakes.

He didn't turn His back on me because I struggled.

His love remained constant.

He was patient.

Merciful.

Faithful.

There were countless moments when He protected me from dangers I didn't even recognize.

There were doors He closed that I wanted opened.

There were situations He kept me from that could have completely changed the course of my life.

When I look back now, I don't see luck.

I see grace.

Amazing grace.

Looking Through the Eyes of Wisdom

As an adult, I don't look back on those years with pride.

Neither do I look back with shame.

I look back with gratitude.

Those experiences remind me of just how patient God has been with me.

They remind me that no one is beyond His reach.

If He could transform a shy, insecure teenage girl searching for acceptance into a woman who now helps others find hope, healing, and financial freedom, then He can do the same for anyone.

My teenage years were not the end of my story.

They were only one chapter.

God was still writing.

Life Lessons

- ❖ *Unhealed wounds often lead to unhealthy choices.*
- ❖ *Temporary pleasures can never satisfy eternal needs.*
- ❖ *Conviction is evidence that God loves us enough to call us higher.*
- ❖ *Peer pressure loses its power when we know our identity.*
- ❖ *God's grace is greater than our mistakes.*
- ❖ *Your past decisions do not cancel God's future purpose.*

Reflection Questions

1. Have you ever sought acceptance in places that left you feeling emptier than before?
2. Can you remember a time when you felt God quietly guiding you away from a wrong decision?
3. What unhealthy habits have you overcome through God's grace?
4. How has God protected you even when you didn't realize it?
5. What would you say to your thirteen-year-old self today?

Chapter Prayer

Heavenly Father,

Thank You for loving me even when I wandered from Your path. Thank You for pursuing me with Your grace when I didn't fully understand Your love.

Forgive me for every decision I made while searching for acceptance in people instead of finding my identity in You. Heal every place in my heart that caused me to seek comfort in things that could never satisfy my soul.

Help me remember that Your plans for my life are greater than any mistake I have ever made. Give me the courage to choose righteousness over popularity, wisdom over impulse, and purpose over temporary pleasure.

I pray for every teenager who is struggling with peer pressure, loneliness, and insecurity. Let them know they are chosen, loved, and created with purpose. Surround them with godly influences and protect them from decisions that could derail their future.

Thank You that You are a God of restoration. Thank You that You redeem our mistakes and use them to build our testimony.

Because of Your grace, I am not defined by my past—I am defined by Your promises.

In Jesus' name,

Amen.

Broken But Not Shattered

by Karen B. Turnage

Chapter 3

Looking for Love

Searching for Acceptance Until I Found the Love That Never Fails

"Delight thyself also in the Lord; and he shall give thee the desires of thine heart."
—Psalm 37:4 (KJV)

By the time I entered young adulthood, I had become an expert at hiding my pain.

On the outside, I smiled.

I laughed.

I made friends.

I appeared confident.

But beneath that smile was a little girl who still longed to be chosen.

Childhood rejection has a way of following you into adulthood if it isn't healed. You begin looking for people to fill places in your heart that only God can fill. Without realizing it, I was searching for someone who would make me feel accepted, valuable, and loved.

What I didn't know then was that love is never meant to become our identity. God intended His love to be our foundation before we ever experience the love of another person.

Looking for Love

After my teenage years, relationships became a significant part of my life. By the age of sixteen or seventeen, I realized that smoking marijuana, partying, and that lifestyle simply were not for me. I knew I wanted something different for my life, even though I didn't yet know what that looked like.

Responsibilities came early.

After graduating from high school at seventeen, my life changed almost overnight. My father was ready to begin a new chapter of his life with his new wife, and living at home was no longer an option. Whether I was ready or not, I was forced to make it on my own.

I found a job at a local convenience store. It was there

that I eventually began a relationship with my manager. When I shared that I was looking for an apartment, he suggested that we move in together. At the time, it seemed like the right decision.

Eventually, we married and started a family. We were blessed with a beautiful baby girl, and I will never forget the excitement we shared when she was born. He was a good husband and a good father.

Looking back, I realize that I was chasing an idea instead of appreciating what God had already given me.

Believing that the grass was greener somewhere else, I made the painful decision to leave my marriage. We divorced, and although I thought I was choosing a better life, I had no idea that I was stepping into one of the most difficult seasons I would ever face.

That's when the real struggle began.

I quickly discovered that I could not afford to live on my own. My desire to be independent collided with the reality of financial hardship. Out of desperation, I found myself moving from one compromising relationship to another simply to survive. I stayed in situations far longer than I should have because I depended on someone else's income to help provide for me and my daughter.

When survival becomes your priority, it's easy to tolerate

things you never imagined you would accept.

I endured lies, cheating, manipulation, broken promises, and emotional abuse. My life was in turmoil.

One relationship became so dangerous that a boyfriend pointed a rifle at my head. Looking back now, I realize how much God protected me during that terrifying moment. The sad reality is that I wasn't even afraid to die. I had become so emotionally exhausted that I had lost sight of my own value.

Another relationship ended when he moved in next door and eventually married another woman. Seeing them together every day became more painful than I could bear, so I moved away just to begin healing.

During that season, I also became pregnant by someone I knew I did not want to spend my life with. Facing one of the hardest decisions of my life, I chose to have an abortion—a decision that brought its own grief, regret, and emotional pain.

Instead of stopping to heal, I continued repeating the same unhealthy patterns, hoping each new relationship would somehow erase the pain of the last.

Like many young women, I dreamed of finding the man who would love me completely. I believed that if someone truly loved me, the emptiness I had carried since childhood would finally disappear. I thought love would silence the feelings of rejection I had lived with for so many years.

Instead, I experienced disappointment.

Some relationships ended because we simply were not meant for one another. Others were built on emotion rather than purpose, chemistry rather than commitment.

Each failed relationship left another scar.

Each goodbye reinforced the questions I had carried since childhood.

"Why doesn't anyone stay?"

"Am I not enough?"

There were even times when I ended relationships before they had the chance to end me. I became so afraid of rejection and abandonment that I would leave first, believing it was easier to walk away than to be left behind. I convinced myself that if I ended the relationship, I could protect my heart from another painful goodbye.

In reality, I wasn't protecting my heart.

I was protecting my wounds.

My fear of heartbreak often kept me from experiencing the very love I longed for.

"What is wrong with me?"

Those questions became louder with every disappointment.

What I didn't realize then was that I was asking imperfect people to heal wounds that only a perfect God could heal. I was searching for validation from people when my true identity had always been found in Christ.

No man could fill the emptiness I carried because that place in my heart was reserved for God alone.

It wasn't until I surrendered my brokenness to Him that I finally discovered that no person could complete me. Only the One who created me could make me whole.

Today, I understand that every painful relationship pointed me toward the greatest relationship I would ever have—a personal relationship with Jesus Christ. He became the love I was searching for, the peace I was longing for, and the healing my heart had desperately needed all along.

I spent years looking for someone to rescue me, only to discover that my Rescuer had been pursuing me all along.

After years of struggling through unhealthy relationships and emotional pain, God blessed me with the opportunity to meet my second husband. To me, he was my knight in shining armor. He was unlike anyone I had ever dated. He was professional, quiet, respectful, laid-back, well-dressed, and carried himself with confidence and integrity. His calm spirit brought stability into my life during a season when I desperately needed it.

Through our marriage, I experienced a different way of living. We traveled together, taking several vacations each year. We enjoyed trying new restaurants, faithfully served together in ministry, and built a wonderful relationship with our blended family. Those years created many beautiful memories that I will always cherish.

Like every marriage, ours had its share of challenges and difficult seasons. We experienced highs and lows, victories and disappointments. After twenty-one years together, we came to the difficult realization that we had grown apart. There was no dramatic event that ended our marriage, no scandal, and no bitterness. We simply reached a place where our paths were no longer leading in the same direction.

By God's grace, we chose to end our marriage with mutual respect, kindness, and dignity. Our divorce was peaceful, and I remain grateful for the years we shared and the lessons we both learned.

That chapter of my life taught me another valuable lesson.

Sometimes, even good seasons come to an end.

Not every ending is the result of failure. Sometimes an ending is simply God's way of making room for a new beginning. Sometimes He closes a chapter so we can fully embrace the purpose He has prepared for the next one.

For me, this was not about running from something. It was about finally running toward the life God had been calling me to live.

For the first time, I wasn't making decisions out of fear, loneliness, or survival. I was making them from a place of healing, maturity, and purpose. I had learned that my identity was no longer found in a relationship, a title, or another person's approval.

My identity was secure in Christ.

I had spent much of my life searching for someone to complete me.

God showed me that **He had already made me complete.**

Looking back now, I can honestly say that every relationship—whether it lasted a few months or many years—taught me something I needed to learn. Some taught me what love looked like. Others taught me what love was not. But every one of them, without exception, pointed me back to God.

He was, and always will be, the greatest love of my life.

The Spirit of Jealousy

One challenge that seemed to follow me throughout my life was dealing with jealousy— mostly from other females.

For years, I couldn't understand it.

I tried to be kind.

I tried to support others.

I celebrated their successes.

I shared opportunities.

I helped others in any way I could.

Yet there always seemed to be someone who misunderstood my intentions, competed with me, or simply didn't like me without really knowing me.

It hurt.

I often wondered why.

As I matured spiritually, God began revealing something to me.

Jealousy is rarely about the person being targeted.

It often comes from wounds in the person who is jealous.

People who are secure don't compete.

People who know their identity don't need to diminish someone else's light.

Understanding that truth helped me stop taking

everything personally.

It also taught me to pray for people instead of becoming bitter toward them.

Rejection Didn't Stop Following Me

Although my surroundings changed, the feeling of rejection often remained.

There were many moments when I felt overlooked. I watched others receive promotions, recognition, and opportunities that I had worked just as hard to earn. I sat through award ceremonies hoping my name would be called, only to leave feeling unseen, disappointed, and empty.

There were also times when I felt excluded from personal celebrations and special occasions. Invitations were extended to others, while I was left wondering why I had not been included. Although those moments may have seemed insignificant to others, they reopened wounds of rejection that had never fully healed.

There were moments when I wondered why I was never the preferred choice. Why did it seem so easy for others to be accepted while I often felt overlooked? Every missed opportunity, every unanswered invitation, and every disappointment seemed to whisper the same familiar lie:

"You're not enough."

For a long time, I allowed those experiences to define my worth. Rejection has a way of making you question your value. It can convince you that you are invisible, unworthy, or somehow lacking. The enemy wants us to believe that if people overlook us, then God must have overlooked us too.

But God was slowly teaching me a life-changing lesson.

Being rejected by people does not mean you have been rejected by God.

In fact, some of God's greatest blessings require Him to close doors that would have kept us from His best. What I once saw as rejection, God was using as protection. The opportunities I didn't receive, the invitations I never got, and the recognition I longed for were not signs that God had forgotten me. They were evidence that He was directing my steps according to His perfect plan.

I came to understand that my value was never determined by a promotion, an award, an invitation, or the approval of others. My worth had already been established by the One who created me. I no longer needed a seat at every table because God had already prepared the table He intended for me. I no longer needed everyone's recognition because I had already been chosen by Him.

Looking back now, I can see that every closed door was

making room for the right one. Every delay was preparing me for God's timing, and every rejection was positioning me for His greater purpose.

Today, I no longer measure my value by who chooses me. I measure it by the fact that **God chose me first**. That truth has given me a peace that no promotion, award, or invitation could ever provide.

Learning to Be Alone

One of the hardest lessons God taught me was learning how to be alone without feeling lonely.

There is a difference.

Loneliness says no one wants you.

Solitude says God is preparing you.

During seasons when relationships ended, I discovered that God often removes distractions so He can speak more clearly.

Those quiet moments became classrooms where He taught me patience.

He taught me discernment.

He taught me that waiting is not punishment.

Waiting is preparation.

God Never Forgot My First Love

When I was thirteen years old, I met a young man (James Turnage, III) who made an impression on my heart.

Even as teenagers, he always treated me like a lady. He showed me kindness, respect, and genuine care in ways that made me feel valued. He gave me a friendship ring and a locket with his picture inside—simple gifts that meant so much to me at the time.

Although we only saw each other occasionally, we cherished the time we spent together. As life took us in different directions, our relationship eventually came to an end. Even so, I have always looked back and reflected on that relationship with gratitude. He set a positive standard for how a young man should treat a young woman and became a wonderful example of what a first boyfriend should be.

Not every relationship is meant to last forever, but some leave lasting lessons. I will always appreciate the respect, kindness, and fond memories we shared during that special season of my life.

Years passed.

We each lived our own lives.

We experienced joys and disappointments.

We grew.

We changed.

I never imagined that God would one day reconnect us.

Only He could orchestrate something so beautiful.

Looking back, I realize that if we had stayed together as teenagers, neither of us would have been ready for the marriage God intended.

We both had growing to do.

Healing to experience.

Lessons to learn.

God wasn't denying me love.

He was preparing both of us for covenant instead of convenience.

His timing was perfect.

God's Definition of Love

Before God restored the relationship that would eventually lead to marriage, He first transformed my understanding of love.

Love is patient.

Love is kind.

Love does not compete.

Love does not manipulate.

Love does not control.

Love is not rooted in fear.

Most importantly, love reflects the character of Christ.

The more I grew spiritually, the more I realized that healthy love begins with a healthy relationship with God.

When we know whose we are, we stop settling for relationships that don't honor who we are.

A New Perspective

Today, I no longer see my failed relationships as failures.

I see them as lessons learned.

As a young single adult, I never looked for a man who had it all together. I wasn't searching for someone with a fancy car, a large bank account, or an impressive title. Instead, I looked for potential. I believed in seeing who a man could become rather than focusing on what he already had.

As long as he treated me with kindness, respect, and had the desire to become better, I was willing to invest in the relationship. I believed in encouraging people to reach their full potential.

Looking back, each relationship—even the ones that ended—taught me something valuable.

Some taught me practical life skills, like basic car repairs. Others exposed me to professionalism and business ownership, inspiring me to think differently about my own future. Other relationships taught me lessons that were even more valuable. They sharpened my ability to discern deception. I learned to recognize lies, manipulation, deceit, infidelity, and empty promises. Over time, God developed within me the gift of discernment.

One thing I can say with confidence is that God protected me from certain relationships. He gave me the ability to recognize drug dealers, drug users, and men who physically abused women. I could sense those warning signs from a mile away, and because of His grace, I never found myself entangled in those kinds of relationships.

That doesn't mean I escaped heartache.

Instead, I encountered a different kind of pain. I had to navigate relationships marked by dishonesty, cheating, manipulation, broken trust, and deceit. Those wounds were often invisible, but they were just as painful. The emotional scars left by betrayal can cut just as deeply as physical wounds.

Looking back, I realize God was protecting me even when I didn't fully understand it. Every disappointment, every broken promise, and every painful lesson was developing my discernment and teaching me not to ignore the warning signs He placed before me.

Today, I thank God for giving me the wisdom to recognize what was unhealthy and the courage to walk away when necessary. What the enemy intended to destroy me, God used to mature me. My experiences taught me that discernment is one of God's greatest gifts. It doesn't just reveal what is wrong—it protects us from what could have been devastating.

Through it all, God saw me through. He never abandoned me, even when I made poor choices or ignored His gentle warnings. His grace covered me, His mercy sustained me, and His hand of protection remained upon my life.

Looking back now, I can truly say that **God's protection was working even before I fully surrendered my life to Him.** That realization alone is a testimony of His unfailing love and faithfulness.

Every relationship became a classroom. Some taught me what love looks like.

Others taught me what love is not.

Some taught me patience.

Others taught me boundaries.

Every experience prepared me for the blessing God had already planned.

Sometimes unanswered prayers become the greatest evidence of God's protection.

Had He answered every prayer I prayed in my younger years, I might have missed the husband He had chosen for me all along.

Only God could take years of disappointment and transform them into a testimony of restoration.

Looking Back with Gratitude

Today I thank God for every "no."

Every closed door.

Every heartbreak.

Every delay.

Every disappointment.

Every failed relationship.

Because each one led me closer to His perfect will.

The little girl who once wondered if she was lovable now knows she has always been deeply loved by her Heavenly Father.

The young woman who searched for acceptance now understands that acceptance was never something she had to earn.

It was a gift from God.

That truth changed everything.

Life Lessons

- ❖ *Never allow another person's rejection to determine your worth.*
- ❖ *God's delays are often His protection.*
- ❖ *A season of singleness can become a season of preparation.*
- ❖ *Jealousy reveals insecurity, not your value.*
- ❖ *Healthy relationships begin with a healthy relationship with God.*
- ❖ *God's timing is always better than our own.*

Reflection Questions

1. Have you ever looked to people to give you what only God could provide?
2. How has rejection shaped your view of yourself?
3. Can you identify relationships that God ended for your protection?
4. What lessons have your disappointments taught you?
5. How has God's timing proven to be better than your own?

Chapter Prayer

Heavenly Father,

Thank You for loving me with an everlasting love. Thank You for reminding me that my worth has never depended on another person's acceptance or rejection.

Heal every wound left by broken relationships. Remove every root of insecurity, fear, loneliness, and disappointment from my heart. Help me forgive those who hurt me and release every painful memory into Your hands.

Teach me to wait on Your timing without becoming discouraged. Give me wisdom to recognize relationships that honor You and the courage to walk away from those that do not.

I pray for every person reading this chapter who feels forgotten, rejected, or unloved. Let them experience the depth of Your unconditional love. Remind them that You have never abandoned them and that Your plans are always for their good.

Thank You for restoring what seemed lost and for proving that Your purpose is greater than my pain. I trust You with my heart, my future, and every relationship You place in my life.

In Jesus' name,

Amen.

Chapter 4

Financial Brokenness

From Bankruptcy to Breakthrough

"But thou shalt remember the Lord thy God: for it is he that giveth thee power to get wealth..."* —*Deuteronomy 8:18 (KJV)

There are some struggles people can see.

Then there are the struggles people never know about.

Financial hardship often falls into the second category.

You can dress well.

Drive a nice car.

Smile at church.

Go to work every day.

Attend family gatherings.

And still go home wondering how you're going to pay your bills.

That was a season of my life.

There were times when I looked successful on the outside while privately carrying the weight of financial stress.

The pressure was exhausting.

Debt has a way of stealing more than money.

It steals peace.

It steals sleep.

It steals confidence.

It steals joy.

It steals hope.

Most of all, it convinces you that you'll never recover.

But the devil is a liar.

God had another plan.

One lesson, however, became crystal clear: **I could not depend on a man to take care of me.**

I discovered that depending on someone else often came with expectations, disappointments, and conditions. That realization awakened something inside of me. It made me desire a better life—not one where I depended on someone else for my security, but one where I could stand on my own two feet and become financially independent.

The struggle, however, was real.

Between the ages of seventeen and thirty-five, life was filled with financial hardship. There were many times when I called family members and friends, believing someone might be able to help. More often than not, I found myself telling my story to four or five different people, reliving my agony and embarrassment over and over again, only to discover that no one was in a position to help.

Most of the time, borrowing money wasn't even an option because I already knew it would only make my financial situation worse. It would simply postpone the problem instead of solving it.

Those were some of the loneliest seasons of my life.

Long before I surrendered my life to Christ, I believed in God. I knew He existed, but I wasn't living for Him. That wouldn't happen until I was thirty-five years old.

Yet even then, when I didn't know Him intimately, I cried out to Him.

I remember standing in the grocery store, carefully watching every dollar I spent. As I approached the checkout, I would ask the cashier for a subtotal, hoping I had enough money to pay for everything. If I didn't, I quietly let the cashier know I would not be getting those items and pretending it didn't bother me.

I remember not being able to shop like everyone else. Shopping for new clothes was a luxury I rarely experienced. Every purchase had to be carefully calculated because every dollar mattered.

There were times when I struggled just to provide food for my daughter and me. There were times I found myself having to choose between cigarettes or lunch while at work. I remember eating hotdogs day after day because they were inexpensive and stretched the little money I had. I remember the kindness of one of my former bosses, who would grocery shop and then bring food to my house so we would have something to eat.

Those acts of kindness meant more than he probably ever realized.

I remember writing a check to cover another, desperately trying to stay one step ahead of my bills. I remember making trips to the bank, hoping I could deposit enough money before checks were returned. I remember receiving utility shutoff notices and lying awake at night wondering how I was going to keep the lights on.

The weight of financial stress was exhausting.

As painful as it is to admit, I also had to confront another truth. Much of my financial hardship wasn't caused solely by my circumstances—it was also the result of my own financial decisions. For years, I lived beyond my means, trying to maintain a lifestyle my income simply couldn't support. I often spent money I didn't have, hoping things would somehow work themselves out.

Eventually, I learned a difficult but necessary lesson: **you cannot build a life of peace on a foundation of poor financial habits.**

God used those years of lack, struggle, and hardship to teach me principles that no classroom ever could. Those painful experiences became the very foundation of my passion for financial stewardship and my desire to help others avoid the mistakes I made.

Today, I don't look back on those years with shame. I look back with gratitude.

They taught me resilience.

They taught me humility.

They taught me compassion.

Most importantly, they taught me that **God is not only interested in saving our souls—He is also interested in transforming our thinking, our habits, and every area of our lives, including our finances.**

Looking back now, I understand that my financial brokenness was never the end of my story. It was simply the beginning of God's restoration.

Living Beyond My Means

Like many people, I made financial decisions without fully understanding the long-term consequences.

Some purchases were based on emotion.

Some were based on convenience.

Some were based on survival.

Some were based on wanting a better life.

Some were trying to look blessed and favoured.

Some were trying to keep up with everyone else.

Others were simply the result of not having enough financial education.

No one teaches most people how to build wealth.

No one teaches budgeting in a practical way.

No one teaches how interest quietly multiplies debt.

No one teaches that every financial decision is connected to your future.

I learned many of those lessons the hard way.

One payment became another.

Credit cards became easier to use than cash.

Unexpected expenses appeared.

Before I realized it, debt had become a lifestyle instead of a temporary situation.

I remember always wanting to drive a new car and live in a nice home—even when I couldn't truly afford either one. On the outside, it appeared that I was doing well, but behind closed doors, I was struggling to keep up with the bills.

As the years went by, I fell into the trap of trying to keep up with everyone else. I charged clothes, shoes, jewelry, and other material things just to create the appearance that I had it all together. I wanted people to think I was successful, when in reality, I was financially broken.

I had mastered the art of looking blessed while secretly being burdened.

The truth is, I was living beyond my means, and every swipe of my credit card only pushed me deeper into debt. I confused possessions with prosperity and appearances with success. I spent money I didn't have to impress people who probably weren't thinking about me at all.

One of the greatest deceptions in our culture—and sometimes even within the church—is believing that our success or God's favour is measured by what we own. We often equate expensive cars, large homes, designer clothes, and luxury items with being blessed.

But I have learned that material possessions are not the true measure of God's blessings.

True wealth is not found in what you can buy. True wealth is found in wisdom, contentment, peace, and good stewardship.

One of the greatest financial lessons God ever taught me is this:

It's not how much money you can spend;
it's how much you can save.

Anyone can spend money.

Wisdom is learning how to manage it.

Building wealth is not about looking rich—it is about making wise decisions that create financial freedom. Looking successful and actually being financially secure are two very different things.

Today, I would rather have money in the bank than designer labels in my closet. I would rather have peace than payments. I would rather build wealth quietly than live a life trying to impress others.

I've learned that financial freedom isn't about having the nicest things—it's about having the freedom to live without the burden of overwhelming debt and the ability to be a blessing to others.

Looking back, I realize God wasn't just changing my financial situation; **He was changing my mindset.** Once my thinking changed, my spending changed. Once my spending changed, my future changed.

Now I understand what I wish I had known years ago:

> ***Don't spend your life trying to look rich.***
> ***Spend your life becoming financially free.***

The Weight of Bankruptcy

There came a point when the burden became too heavy to carry.

After much thought and many sleepless nights, I made one of the hardest financial decisions of my life.

I filed for bankruptcy.

That word alone carries so much shame.

For a long time, I felt embarrassed, ashamed and defeated.

I wondered what people would think if they knew.

I questioned myself.

"How did I get here?"

"Did I fail?"

"Will I ever recover?"

Bankruptcy felt like the end.

But it wasn't.

It was simply a reset.

One of the greatest lies the enemy tells us is that our failures define us.

God reminded me that bankruptcy was an event.

It was never my identity.

I wasn't bankrupt.

I had gone through bankruptcy.

There is a difference.

God Was Teaching Me Stewardship

As painful as that season was, it became one of the greatest classrooms of my life.

God wasn't interested in simply giving me more money.

He first wanted to change the way I thought about money.

He taught me that stewardship is more important than income.

You can earn six figures and still live paycheck to paycheck.

You can receive promotions and still have no peace.

Without wisdom, more money simply creates bigger problems.

God began changing my mindset.

Instead of asking, "How much can I spend?"

I started asking, "How can I honor God with what He has already given me?"

That question changed everything. I started getting more excited to SAVE rather than spending.

Creating a Debt Freedom Plan

I knew I couldn't continue living the way I had before.

If I wanted different results, I had to make different decisions.

So I created something that would eventually change my life forever—in 2020

A Debt Freedom Plan.

It wasn't complicated.

It was consistent.

I created a 12 Month budget.

I tracked every dollar.

I distinguished between needs and wants.

I stopped trying to impress people.

I learned to delay gratification.

I became intentional instead of emotional.

Little by little...

Payment by payment...

Decision by decision...

Freedom began replacing fear.

There were moments when progress felt slow.

There were times when I wanted to quit.

But every debt I paid reminded me that I was getting closer to the life God had promised.

Renewing My Mind

The greatest transformation wasn't happening in my bank account.

It was happening in my mind.

I no longer believed that debt was normal.

I no longer believed I had to keep up with everyone else.

I no longer measured success by what I owned.

God taught me that real wealth is having peace.

Real wealth is sleeping at night.

Real wealth is living **beneath** your means.

Real wealth is having the freedom to obey God without financial fear.

That was a richer life than any paycheck could provide.

Nobody But God

As the years passed, something remarkable happened.

The same woman who once struggled under the weight of debt began experiencing financial restoration.

Not overnight.

Not through luck.

Not by winning the lottery.

But through God's wisdom, discipline, obedience, and grace.

Today I look around and see evidence of His faithfulness everywhere.

Four debt-free automobiles.

Two beautiful, fully appointed homes.

Businesses that provide opportunities to serve others.

The ability to help people who once stood where I stood.

This isn't a story about material possessions.

It's a story about God's restoration.

Every vehicle reminds me where He brought me from.

Every home reminds me of His promises.

Every blessing reminds me that obedience produces fruit.

When people ask me how I made it…

My answer is simple.

Nobody but God.

Why I Became a Financial Coach

My financial journey wasn't just about me.

God rarely blesses us only for ourselves.

He blesses us so we can become a blessing.

The lessons I learned through debt, discipline, and restoration became the foundation of my calling.

Today I have the privilege of helping others create budgets, eliminate debt, rebuild their finances, and discover financial freedom.

I don't teach theory.

I teach testimony.

I know what it's like to struggle and feel overwhelmed.

I know what it's like to start over.

I know what it's like to wonder if things will ever change.

That's why I can look people in the eye and confidently tell them: **"If God did it for me, He can do it for you."**

Abundant Living

Jesus said in John 10:10:

> ***"I am come that they might have life, and that they might have it more abundantly."***

For years, I misunderstood that verse.

I thought abundance was about having more.

Now I understand that abundance is about living in the fullness of God's will.

Abundance is peace.

Abundance is wisdom.

Abundance is contentment.

Abundance is generosity.

Abundance is freedom.

God didn't simply deliver me from debt.

He delivered me from the mindset that created debt.

That is true freedom.

Life Lessons

- *Bankruptcy is an event—not your identity.*
- *Financial freedom begins with changing your mindset.*
- *Discipline creates the life that emotions cannot.*

- *Delayed gratification produces lasting rewards.*
- *Stewardship invites God's increase.*
- *God can restore every area surrendered to Him.*
- *Your testimony becomes someone else's roadmap to freedom.*

Reflection Questions

1. What financial habits are preventing you from experiencing freedom?
2. Do you view money as a tool or as your source of security?
3. What changes can you make today to become a better steward?
4. Have you allowed shame from past financial mistakes to define you?
5. How can your testimony encourage someone else who is struggling financially?

Chapter Prayer

Heavenly Father,

Thank You for being Jehovah Jireh, my Provider. Thank You for never abandoning me during seasons of lack and for teaching me that true riches are found in Your wisdom.

Forgive me for every financial decision that was driven by

fear, pride, impatience, or lack of knowledge. Help me become a faithful steward of every resource You place in my hands.

Break every cycle of debt, financial bondage, and poverty thinking. Replace fear with faith, anxiety with peace, and confusion with wisdom. Teach me to manage money in a way that honors You and blesses future generations.

I pray for every reader carrying the burden of financial stress. Give them hope where they see hopelessness, direction where they see confusion, and courage to take the first step toward financial freedom.

Thank You that bankruptcy is not the end of anyone's story. Thank You that You specialize in restoration. May every financial victory point people back to You so they will know that every good and perfect gift comes from above.

I declare that I will live in wisdom, generosity, contentment, and abundance—not because of my own strength, but because of Your grace. In Jesus' name, **Amen.**

Broken But Not Shattered

by Karen B. Turnage

Chapter 5

Purpose Born from Pain

When God Turns Your Broken Pieces into Your Greatest Gifts

"And we know that all things work together for good to them that love God, to them who are the called according to His purpose."
—Romans 8:28 (KJV)

As I look back over my life, one thing has become abundantly clear:

Nothing God allows is ever wasted.

There were seasons when I believed I was simply trying to survive. I couldn't understand why my life seemed filled with detours, disappointments, temporary jobs, failed relationships, financial struggles, and constant change.

I often wondered, *"Lord, what are You doing?"*

What I couldn't see then was that every experience was a classroom.

Every challenge was a lesson.

Every disappointment was preparation.

God wasn't delaying my purpose.

He was developing me for it.

Every Job Had a Purpose

There was a time when I worked one temporary assignment after another.

At first, I questioned why I couldn't seem to find stability.

I watched other people settle into long-term careers while I packed boxes, learned new offices, met new supervisors, and adapted to new environments.

I wondered if something was wrong with me.

But God knew exactly what He was doing.

Every assignment taught me something different.

One job sharpened my administrative skills.

Another strengthened my communication.

Another taught me professionalism.

Another developed patience.

Another showed me how to work with people from different backgrounds and personalities.

At the time, I thought I was simply earning a paycheck.

In reality, God was building a leader.

Government Service

My journey eventually led me to positions with the Department of Social Services (DCSE) and Richmond Redevelopment & Housing Authority.

These opportunities opened my eyes to the realities many families face every day.

I met people who were struggling financially.

Families searching for stability.

Individuals trying to rebuild their lives after devastating setbacks.

Instead of judging them, I understood them.

Pain has a way of creating compassion.

Because I had experienced brokenness myself, I could see people through eyes of grace rather than criticism.

Those jobs taught me something that no college course ever could.

Everyone has a story.

The person asking for help today may simply be one

opportunity away from changing their entire life.

That truth has stayed with me ever since.

Mt. Gilead Full Gospel International Ministries

"The Home of Overcomers"

A Divine Assignment

On June 30th of 2003, God opened a door that would forever change the course of my life. He blessed me with the opportunity to work in the Administrative Offices of ***Mt. Gilead Full Gospel International Ministries*** in ***Chesterfield, Virginia*** under the leadership of Bishop Daniel Robertson, Jr and CoPastor Elena Robertson, where I began serving as an Administrative Assistant.

In that role, I wore many hats. I designed and produced church bulletins and other ministry materials, recorded voice-overs for church announcements, counted tithes and offerings, proofread documents and provided administrative support wherever it was needed. Although the work was demanding, I embraced every opportunity to learn and grow. Looking back, I can see that every assignment was preparing me for something much greater than I could have imagined.

Two years later, I was promoted to ***Financial Administrator***, a position that would become one of the greatest learning experiences of my professional career.

Again, I found myself stepping into responsibilities that I

had never been formally trained to perform. Yet God continued to equip me every step of the way. What I lacked in experience, He supplied through wisdom, favor, discernment, and a teachable spirit. Every challenge became another opportunity to witness His faithfulness.

For the next twelve years, I had the privilege of helping develop and strengthen the ministry's financial operations. I created and implemented budgeting and financial reporting systems, processed payroll, prepared financial statements, managed accounts payable and accounts receivable, performed bank reconciliations and general ledger adjustments, monitored cash flow, coordinated department budgets and salary updates, ensured compliance with payroll tax regulations, and assisted with Human Resources.

I was especially grateful for the opportunity to be a part of the journey of paying off our church's mortgage of $1.6 million in a record time rally of 3 months and 1 week! Glory to God!!

Every responsibility sharpened my knowledge, strengthened my work ethic, and increased my confidence.

At the time, I thought I was simply building a career.

Looking back now, I realize God was building **me**.

While I was helping the ministry establish sound financial systems, God was quietly establishing financial order in my own life. The same budgeting principles, accountability, organization, and stewardship that I practiced each day at work began transforming my personal finances. I learned how to create and follow a budget, pay my bills on time, live within my means, and become a better steward of the resources God had entrusted to me. From God's House to My House!

For years, I had struggled with poor financial decisions and the desire to appear successful rather than become financially secure. But through this experience, God began renewing my mindset. He showed me that financial freedom is not built by how much money you make, but by how faithfully you manage what He has already placed in your hands.

That twelve-year season was truly an opportunity of a lifetime. It not only equipped me with invaluable professional skills, but it also laid the foundation for the work God would later call me to do through **Abundant Living Community Services**, where I now have the privilege of teaching others the very financial principles that transformed my own life.

Today, I understand that every spreadsheet I created, every budget I balanced, every payroll I processed, and every financial report I prepared was part of God's training ground.

I also understand something else: **God doesn't always call the qualified; He qualifies those He calls.**

Without a college degree or prior experience, He revealed gifts, talents, and abilities that had been hidden inside of me all along. He proved that when He opens a door, no lack of credentials can stop His purpose from being fulfilled.

He wasn't just preparing me to manage finances.

He was preparing me to transform lives.

Discovering Gifts I Never Knew I Had

As the years passed, God continued revealing gifts that had been hidden inside me all along.

I became fascinated with numbers.

Finance Accounting became more than a job.

It became a way of bringing order where there had once been confusion.

Then came Graphic Design.

Website development.

Creative writing.

Playwriting.

Mobile Notary/Loan Signing Agent.

A Realtor.

Financial Coaching.

Business ownership.

A Group Home Provider & Consultant.

Each new opportunity seemed completely different from the one before.

People often asked me, "How do you do so many different things?"

The answer was simple.

I didn't give myself those gifts.

God did.

He had been developing them throughout my entire life.

But every one of those gifts was born through seasons of learning, sacrifice, mistakes, perseverance, and faith.

None of them happened overnight.

Each one represents another example of God's faithfulness.

I have learned that God rarely gives us gifts for our own benefit alone.

He gives us gifts so we can serve others.

The more faithfully we serve, the more opportunities He entrusts to us.

Brokenness Created Compassion

One of the greatest gifts that came from my painful experiences was compassion.

Because I understood rejection, I could encourage the rejected.

Because I understood financial struggle, I could teach financial freedom.

Because I understood starting over, I could help others rebuild.

Because I knew what it felt like to question my worth, I could remind others of theirs.

God never intended for my pain to remain private.

He intended for it to become someone else's breakthrough.

The wounds that once embarrassed me became the very places where God's healing power could shine.

My Calling as a Financial Coach

Of all the roles God has allowed me to serve in, becoming a Financial Coach has been one of the most rewarding.

Why?

Because I don't teach from theory.

I teach from experience.

I've felt the pressure of debt.

I've experienced the embarrassment of bankruptcy.

I've lived through financial uncertainty.

I've also experienced the joy of becoming debt free.

That gives me credibility no textbook could ever provide.

When I encourage someone to stay disciplined, I know what discipline costs.

When I tell them debt freedom is possible, I'm speaking from personal experience.

When I say, "Don't quit," I remember the days I wanted to quit myself.

My testimony became my teaching.

Becoming a Group Home Provider & Consultant

Another chapter of God's purpose **continues to unfold as He has led me into serving individuals with intellectual disabilities through group home care.**

This isn't simply another business venture.

It is ministry.

I continue to learn that every person deserves dignity. Every person deserves compassion. Every person deserves to be seen, heard, respected, and given the opportunity to live a meaningful life.

As I work with individuals who need additional support, I recognize something familiar. Many of them, like me, simply want someone to believe in them—someone to encourage them, advocate for them, celebrate their accomplishments, and remind them that their lives matter.

That realization continues to touch my heart deeply.

My responsibility is about much more than providing a home or meeting someone's basic needs. I want the individuals I serve to experience belonging, independence, personal growth, meaningful relationships, and the joy of knowing they are valued.

God continues to expand this purpose beyond the individuals I serve. He gives me the opportunity to **mentor and coach other group home providers**, sharing my knowledge and experiences while helping others understand how they, too, can become providers and make a difference in someone's life.

I realize that God isn't only calling me to serve—He is calling me to **teach others how to serve**.

What begins as an opportunity continues to become another extension of my purpose.

My experiences continue to teach me that purpose is never just about making money. There is nothing wrong with building a successful business, but true success is measured by more than income. It is also measured by **impact**.

How many people do you encourage?
How many lives do you help improve?
How many people discover possibilities because you believe in them?
How many others do you teach to become a blessing?

For me, group home care is another example of how God takes the broken pieces of my own life and uses them to help me recognize the value in someone else's.

Purpose is about making a difference.

It is about using what God has placed in your hands to enrich and empower the lives of others. And sometimes, your greatest assignment is simply helping another person understand:

You matter. You have value. Your life has meaning. And you deserve the opportunity to live it abundantly.

Your Pain Has a Purpose

If there is one lesson my life has taught me, it is this:

Your pain is never pointless.

The very thing you wish had never happened may become the very thing God uses to change someone else's life.

My rejection taught me compassion.

My financial struggles taught me stewardship.

My broken relationships taught me discernment.

My temporary jobs taught me adaptability.

My failures taught me humility.

My faith taught me perseverance.

Nothing was wasted.

Nothing.

God was weaving every chapter together into a story only He could write.

Nobody But God

Sometimes people ask me how I learned to do so many different things.

I smile because they assume it was talent alone.

The truth is much deeper.

Every skill came through a season.

Every opportunity came through obedience.

Every success came through God's grace.

When I think about where I started—a shy little girl carrying the weight of rejection—and compare it to where God has brought me today, I can only say three words:

Nobody But God!

Life Lessons

- *God never wastes your experiences.*
- *Temporary seasons often prepare us for permanent assignments.*
- *Your greatest ministry may come from your deepest pain.*
- *Every gift God gives you has a purpose beyond yourself.*
- *Compassion grows through personal experience.*
- *Faithfulness in small assignments prepares you for greater ones.*
- *Your testimony is one of your greatest qualifications.*

Reflection Questions

1. Looking back, where can you see God preparing you through difficult seasons?
2. What gifts has God placed inside you that you may have overlooked?
3. How has your pain increased your compassion for others?
4. What experiences in your life could become part of someone else's healing?
5. Are you willing to let God use every part of your story for His glory?

Chapter Prayer

Heavenly Father,

Thank You for proving that nothing in my life has been wasted. Every disappointment, every detour, every temporary assignment, and every painful season has become part of the beautiful story You are writing.

Help me never despise small beginnings or ordinary opportunities. Teach me to be faithful wherever You place me, knowing that You are preparing me for greater purpose.

Thank You for every gift You have entrusted to me. May I use my talents—not for personal recognition—but to glorify You and serve others with excellence, humility, and compassion.

I pray for every reader who feels overlooked, uncertain, or discouraged. Reveal the purpose hidden within their pain. Open their eyes to the gifts You have placed inside them and give them the courage to walk boldly in their calling.

Lord, let my life always point back to You. May every accomplishment, every business, every opportunity, and every success be a testimony that You are the One who equips, empowers, and promotes.

Thank You for taking the broken pieces of my life and creating something beautiful for Your Kingdom.

I surrender my gifts, my purpose, and my future completely to You. In Jesus' name, **Amen.**

Broken But Not Shattered

by Karen B. Turnage

Chapter 6

The Turning Point

When I Found Christ, I Found Myself

"Therefore, if any man be In Christ, he is a new creature: old things are passed away; behold, all things are become new."
—2 Corinthians 5:17 (KJV)

If someone were to ask me what changed my life the most, my answer would not be a career, a business, a home, or even financial freedom.

It would be one simple answer:

Jesus.

Everything I had experienced up to that point—childhood rejection, broken relationships, financial struggles, temporary jobs, and searching for acceptance—had prepared me for one divine appointment.

God was calling me to Himself.

Looking back now, I realize that every painful season had been leading me toward His grace.

A Divine Appointment

One of the greatest blessings God ever gave me was leading me to **Mt. Gilead Full Gospel International Ministries in March of 1999**. I didn't realize it at the time, but God was about to completely change the direction of my life.

That same year, in honor of my father on Father's Day and because of my newfound respect and desire to live for God, I made the decision to quit smoking cigarettes. I had tried to quit numerous times before without success, but this time was different. I quit **cold turkey**.

Whenever the urge to smoke came over me, I reached for my Bible instead of a cigarette. I would read the Word of God until the craving passed. The Bible became my source of strength, and God's Word sustained me when my own willpower wasn't enough.

What I had been unable to accomplish through repeated attempts, **God gave me the strength to overcome and took away the desire. Glory to God!!!**

On **July 4, 1999**, I officially became a member of Mt. Gilead. Looking back, I can't help but recognize the significance of that date. July 4th represents freedom, and in many ways, I was beginning to experience a new kind of freedom of my own—freedom in Christ.

Walking through the doors of Mt. Gilead was about much more than attending another church.

It was the beginning of a completely new life.

For the first time, I began to understand who God truly was—not simply as the God I had heard about growing up, but as a God I could know personally.

The God who loved **me**.

The God who had never abandoned **me**.

The God who had protected **me**, even during the years when I wasn't fully living for Him.

The God who had watched over me through childhood rejection, difficult relationships, financial struggles, poor decisions, heartbreak, and every season when I didn't know how I was going to make it.

Most importantly, I began to understand that God had a **purpose for every chapter of my life**—even the chapters I wished I could erase.

What I once considered wasted years, God would eventually use as wisdom. What I considered mistakes,

He would use as lessons. What I considered brokenness, He would ultimately transform into testimony.

I had spent so much of my life searching for acceptance, love, security, and a place where I truly belonged.

And when I finally developed a personal relationship with God, I realized something beautiful:

I had finally come home.

Learning Under Great Leadership

At Mt. Gilead FGIM, The Home of Overcomers—

I had the privilege of sitting under the teaching of ***Bishop Daniel Robertson, Jr. and CoPastor Elena Robertson***

Their teaching challenged me to grow beyond religion and develop a genuine relationship with God.

Week after week, I learned truths that transformed my thinking.

I learned that salvation was not just about going to heaven.

It was about living a victorious life here on earth.

I learned that God desired a relationship with me.

I learned that His Word was alive.

I learned that His promises were still true.

Most importantly, I learned that God is faithful.

Those teachings became the foundation upon which I would build the rest of my life.

Renewing My Mind

Before God could change my circumstances, He had to change my thinking.

For years I had believed lies.

I believed I wasn't enough.

I believed rejection defined me.

I believed financial struggle was simply part of my future.

I believed I had to prove my worth.

God's Word confronted every one of those beliefs.

Romans 12:2 became more than a scripture.

It became a lifestyle.

The more I studied God's Word, the more my thinking changed.

Fear gave way to faith.

Doubt gave way to confidence.

Scarcity gave way to abundance.

Shame gave way to purpose.

My life didn't change overnight.

But my mind did.

And once my mind changed, my decisions began to change.

Those new decisions eventually changed my life.

Learning About God's Goodness

One of the greatest revelations I received was understanding the goodness of God.

Through His Word, I discovered a loving Father.

A Father who delights in blessing His children.

A Father who forgives.

A Father who restores.

A Father who heals.

A Father who provides.

I began to understand that God wasn't waiting for me to fail.

He was waiting for me to trust Him.

That revelation removed fear from my relationship with Him.

Instead of serving Him out of obligation, I began serving Him out of love.

Understanding His Benefits

Psalm 103 became one of my favorite passages of Scripture.

It reminds us not to forget all of God's benefits.

He forgives.

He heals.

He redeems.

He crowns us with lovingkindness.

He satisfies us with good things.

Those weren't just words on a page.

They became my testimony.

I watched God restore areas of my life that I thought would remain broken forever.

He healed my heart.

He strengthened my faith.

He gave me wisdom.

He restored my finances.

He gave me peace.

His benefits were real.

Seeing God's Manifestations

As my faith grew, I began witnessing God's hand in ways I had never noticed before.

Doors opened that no person could have opened.

Opportunities appeared that I could never have arranged

on my own.

Divine connections came into my life.

Favour surrounded me.

Provision arrived at exactly the right time.

God's presence became undeniable.

The more obedient I became, the more I recognized His fingerprints on every area of my life.

His manifestations weren't simply miracles.

They were evidence that He was actively involved in my journey.

Faith Requires Obedience

One lesson I learned early was that faith is more than believing.

Faith obeys.

There were times God instructed me to trust Him when it made no sense.

There were opportunities that required courage.

There were decisions that required sacrifice.

Sometimes obedience felt uncomfortable.

Sometimes it required waiting.

Sometimes it meant saying no when everyone else was saying yes.

But every act of obedience strengthened my relationship with God.

Every step of faith prepared me for the next blessing.

Looking back now, I understand that delayed obedience would have delayed many of God's blessings in my life.

Becoming the Woman God Created Me to Be

Little by little, God transformed me.

The shy little girl began speaking with confidence.

The rejected child became a woman who knew she was chosen.

The financially broken woman became a faithful steward.

The woman who questioned her value became someone who now helps others discover theirs.

The more time I spent in God's presence, the more I became the woman He had always intended me to be.

Not perfect.

But growing.

Not without challenges.

But never without hope.

Nobody But God

Sometimes people only see the results.

They see the businesses.

They see the homes.

They see the debt-free automobiles.

They see the accomplishments.

They don't see the prayers.

The tears.

The sacrifices.

The discipline.

The countless hours spent studying & meditating on God's Word.

The lessons learned under Godly leadership.

Everything I am today began with one decision:

To give my life completely to Jesus Christ.

Without Him, none of this would exist.

Absolutely none of it.

Nobody but God!

Life Lessons

- *A relationship with Jesus changes everything.*
- *True transformation begins with renewing your mind.*
- *God's Word has the power to replace every lie with truth.*
- *Obedience opens the door to God's blessings.*

- *God's goodness is experienced through a relationship, not just religion.*
- *Spiritual growth is a lifelong journey.*
- *Everything God restores should point others back to Him.*

Reflection Questions

1. What lies have you believed about yourself that God's Word can replace?
2. How has God used spiritual mentors to shape your life?
3. In what areas is God asking you to trust Him more deeply?
4. How have you experienced God's goodness in difficult seasons?
5. What step of obedience is God asking you to take today?

Chapter Prayer

Heavenly Father,

Thank You for calling me to Yourself and for never giving up on me. Thank You for pursuing me with Your love, even when I was searching for fulfillment in other places.

Thank You for the gift of salvation and for transforming

my life through Your Son, Jesus Christ. Thank You for leading me to a place where I could grow in Your Word, deepen my faith, and discover who You created me to be.

Renew my mind daily through Your truth. Remove every lie, every fear, and every limitation that does not align with Your Word. Help me walk by faith and not by sight, trusting that Your plans for my life are always good.

Thank You for every spiritual leader, teacher, and mentor You have placed in my life. Bless them for their faithfulness and continue to use them to advance Your Kingdom.

I pray for every reader who longs for a fresh start. Let them experience the same transforming power that changed my life. Draw them into a deeper relationship with You, heal every broken place, and remind them that no life is beyond Your ability to restore.

May everything I accomplish bring glory to Your name. Let my life always testify that every blessing, every victory, and every breakthrough came from You.

For truly, **Nobody But God!**

In the mighty name of Jesus, **Amen.**

Chapter 7

Living the Abundant Life

From Surviving to Thriving—A Life Only God Could Build

"The thief cometh not, but for to steal, and to kill, and to destroy: I am come that they might have life, and that they might have it more abundantly."
—John 10:10 (KJV)

There was a time in my life when simply making it through the month felt like a victory.

Paying the bills on time was a celebration.

Avoiding another collection notice was a relief.

Finding enough money to cover an unexpected expense felt like a miracle. Those days taught me humility.

They also taught me dependence upon God.

Today, when I look around at the life God has entrusted to me, I am overwhelmed—not because of what I own, but because I know where He brought me from.

Everything I have is a testimony of His faithfulness.

Abundance Looks Different Now

When I was younger in Christ, I thought abundance meant having more possessions.

More money.

A nicer house.

A better car.

But God taught me that abundance begins long before material blessings arrive.

Abundance begins with peace.

It begins with contentment.

It begins with knowing that your needs are met because your Father is your Provider.

Material blessings are simply the overflow of faithful stewardship.

God first taught me how to manage little before He entrusted me with much.

That lesson changed my entire perspective.

The Debt Freedom Journey

Becoming debt free wasn't one big moment.

It was thousands of small decisions.

Choosing discipline over impulse.

Choosing wisdom over emotion.

Choosing saving instead of spending.

Choosing contentment instead of comparison.

Every financial decision became an act of obedience.

Every dollar received became an opportunity to honor God.

Every debt that disappeared strengthened my confidence that God's principles truly work.

Eventually, what once seemed impossible became reality.

Debt no longer controlled my life.

Fear no longer controlled my decisions.

Freedom had become my new normal.

Living What I Teach

One of the greatest joys of my life is knowing that I don't simply encourage others to pursue financial freedom—I have lived the journey myself.

When I teach budgeting, I remember creating my own.

When I encourage someone to stay disciplined, I remember the sacrifices.

When I tell a family not to lose hope, I remember the days when I needed hope myself.

That is why I believe testimony is one of God's greatest teaching tools.

People don't simply need information.

They need proof that transformation is possible.

God allowed me to experience breakthrough so I could help someone else experience theirs.

A Legacy of Stewardship

Today, I thank God for allowing me to own four debt-free luxury automobiles.

Not because they define my success.

But because they remind me of His faithfulness.

I thank Him for two beautiful, fully appointed homes.

Not because houses make me valuable.

But because they stand as monuments to His promises.

Every room reminds me that God restores.

Every key reminds me that obedience matters.

Every blessing reminds me that He is still a covenant-keeping God.

Years ago, I never imagined I would be in this position.

Yet here I am.

Not because I am extraordinary.

But because God is.

Success with Purpose

God never intended prosperity to become my destination.

He intended it to become my **platform**.

The businesses He has entrusted to me are opportunities to serve.

My work as a Financial Coach allows me to help families escape financial bondage.

My work as a Group Home Provider allows me to care for individuals with dignity and compassion.

Every client.

Every family.

Every life I touch.

Every opportunity to encourage someone.

Those are the true rewards.

Money can purchase many things.

But it cannot purchase purpose.

Purpose comes from God.

The Blessing of Generosity

One unexpected blessing of financial freedom is the ability to give.

Matthew 6:38 KJV: Give, and it shall be given, unto you: good measure, pressed down, and shaken together, and running over, shall men give into your bosom.

There was a time when I wished I could help others but simply didn't have the resources.

Today, God has blessed me to become a blessing.

Whether encouraging someone through coaching, helping a family in need, supporting ministry, or investing in another person's future, I have discovered that generosity is one of the greatest joys of abundance.

God never blesses us simply to increase our standard of living.

He blesses us so we can increase our standard of giving to include Tithes & Offerings.

God reminded me that I have purchased 4 debt free automobiles for others and He has rewarded me the same!

The more He entrusted to me, the more I realized that I owned nothing.

Everything belongs to Him.

I am simply the manager.

Staying Humble

Success has a way of testing your character.

It is easy to become prideful when people admlre your accomplishments.

But every time someone congratulates me, I remember where I came from.

I remember the bankruptcy.

I remember the rejection.

I remember the temporary jobs.

I remember the nights of uncertainty.

I remember the prayers.

I remember the tears.

I remember how many times God carried me when I

couldn't carry myself.

I remember the overall struggle. It was REAL!

That keeps me humble.

Without Him, none of this would exist.

Nobody But God

People sometimes ask, "How did you do it?"

My answer is always the same.

Nobody but God!

It wasn't luck.

It wasn't perfect timing.

It wasn't because I was smarter than anyone else.

It was God's grace.

His wisdom.

His favour.

His mercy.

His discipline working in my life.

Everything I have today is evidence that God still restores broken people.

He still heals wounded hearts.

He still delivers people from debt.

He still opens doors no one can shut.

He still fulfills His promises.

And He is still writing testimonies.

Mine is simply one of them.

Living with Eternal Perspective

The greatest lesson abundance has taught me is this:

Everything I own is temporary.

My homes will one day belong to someone else.

My automobiles will eventually wear out.

Businesses will change.

Careers will end.

But the lives touched through obedience will last forever.

That is the legacy I want to leave.

Not simply that I accumulated wealth.

But that I used every blessing to glorify God, strengthen families, encourage the discouraged, and point people toward Jesus Christ.

That is the Abundant Life.

Life Lessons

- *Financial freedom begins with faithful stewardship.*
- *True abundance starts in the heart before it appears in the bank account.*
- *Success is a platform for serving others.*

- *Every blessing should point back to God.*
- *Generosity is one of the greatest signs of spiritual maturity.*
- *Stay humble enough to remember where God brought you from.*
- *Your greatest legacy is the lives you influence for Christ.*

Reflection Questions

1. How do you define abundance?
2. Are you managing what God has already entrusted to you faithfully?
3. In what ways can your success become a blessing to others?
4. How has God demonstrated His faithfulness in your own life?
5. What legacy are you building that will outlive you?

Chapter Prayer

Heavenly Father,

Thank You for Your abundant blessings and for teaching me that true prosperity begins with a heart surrendered to You. Thank You for every lesson learned through seasons of lack and every victory experienced through faithful obedience.

Keep me humble as You continue to bless me. Never allow success to replace my dependence on You. Help me remember that everything I have belongs to You and has been entrusted to me for Your purposes.

Teach me to be a faithful steward, a generous giver, and a willing servant. May my businesses, my home, my resources, and every opportunity You provide become instruments that bring glory to Your name and hope to others.

I pray for every reader who longs to experience financial freedom and the abundant life You promised. Give them wisdom to make sound decisions, courage to remain disciplined, and faith to trust You during every season.

May they discover, as I have, that abundance is not measured by possessions alone, but by peace, purpose, contentment, and a life fully surrendered to Christ.

Thank You for proving that You are still in the business of restoring broken lives, healing wounded hearts, and blessing those who faithfully follow You.

And may every blessing, every achievement, and every victory forever declare these simple but powerful words:

Nobody But God. In Jesus' mighty name, **Amen.**

Broken But Not Shattered

by Karen B. Turnage

Chapter 8

Broken But Not Shattered

The Beauty of God's Restoration

> ***"And I will restore to you the years that the locust hath eaten..."***
> ***—Joel 2:25 (KJV)***

As I sit and reflect on my life's journey, I cannot help but smile.

Not because every chapter was easy.

Not because I never cried.

Not because I never questioned God.

I smile because I now understand something I couldn't see while I was living through it.

God was never absent.

Even when I couldn't trace His hand, I could trust His heart.

Looking back, every chapter of my life has one common thread.

God's faithfulness.

The Broken Little Girl

I remember the little girl who wondered why she wasn't raised by her biological mother.

The little girl who questioned her worth.

The little girl who felt different.

The little girl who struggled to find her place in a blended family.

She didn't know it then, but God was holding her every step of the way.

Although I felt broken, I was never abandoned.

Although I felt rejected, I was never forgotten.

Although I cried many tears, Heaven never stopped watching over me.

Today, I wish I could sit beside that little girl and whisper into her ear,

"You're going to make it."

"God has an incredible plan for your life."

"Don't give up."

"The pain won't last forever."

"One day, your story will become someone else's hope."

Every Chapter Had a Purpose

When I think about my teenage years, I no longer focus only on the mistakes.

I see God's mercy.

When I remember failed relationships, I no longer focus only on heartbreak.

I see His protection.

When I think about bankruptcy, I no longer remember embarrassment.

I remember the beginning of wisdom.

When I think about temporary jobs, I don't remember instability.

I remember preparation.

When I think about my salvation and spiritual growth, I don't simply remember attending church.

I remember meeting the Savior who changed everything.

Every chapter had a purpose.

Every season had a lesson.

Every delay had a reason.

Nothing was wasted.

God Restored More Than My Finances

People often celebrate the visible blessings.

The debt-free automobiles.

The beautiful homes.

The successful businesses.

The opportunities.

The accomplishments.

Those blessings are wonderful.

But they are not God's greatest miracle in my life.

His greatest miracle was restoring my heart.

He healed the rejection.

He healed the loneliness.

He healed the fear.

He healed the insecurity.

He healed the shame.

He restored my confidence.

He restored my hope.

He restored my faith.

Because once God heals your heart, everything else begins to change.

The Meaning of Success

The world often measures success by titles, income, influence, and possessions.

God measures success differently.

Success is obedience.

Success is faithfulness.

Success is serving others with love.

Success is remaining humble when God elevates you.

Success is pointing people to Christ instead of yourself.

If my life encourages one person to trust God...

If one family chooses financial freedom...

If one woman realizes she is enough...

If one teenager walks away from destructive choices...

If one person discovers Jesus because of my testimony...

Then every painful season was worth it.

My Greatest Accomplishment

Over the years, I have worn many titles.

Daughter.

Mother.

Wife.

Financial Coach.

Financial Accountant.

Graphic Designer.

Playwright.

Mobile Notary & Loan Signing Agent.

Business Owner.

Group Home Provider and Consultant.

Realtor.

And now an aspired Author & Publisher.

Each title represents a season.

Each one is a blessing.

But none of those titles define who I am.

My greatest accomplishment is simply this:

I belong to Jesus Christ.

Everything else flows from that relationship.

Without Him, there would be no testimony.

Without Him, there would be no restoration.

Without Him, there would be no abundant life.

My Message to the Broken

If you are reading this book while carrying pain...

Please hear my heart.

You are not forgotten.

You are not disqualified.

You are not too broken.

You are not too late.

Your mistakes do not have the final word.

Your diagnosis does not have the final word.

Your bankruptcy does not have the final word.

Your rejection does not have the final word.

God does.

Your current chapter is not your final chapter.

The Author of your life is still writing.

Trust Him.

What I Have Learned

If I could summarize everything God has taught me, it would be this:

Forgive quickly.

Love deeply.

Serve faithfully.

Give generously.

Trust completely.

Pray continually.

Obey immediately.

Never stop believing.

God is faithful.

He has never failed me.

Not once.

Sometimes His answer was "yes."

Sometimes His answer was "wait."

Sometimes His answer was "I have something better."

Looking back now, every answer was perfect.

Nobody But God

People occasionally ask how I overcame rejection.

How I recovered from financial hardship.

How I rebuilt after bankruptcy.

How I discovered purpose.

How I found peace.

How I became financially free.

How I own debt-free automobiles.

How I own beautiful homes.

How I built successful businesses.

How I continue helping others.

I simply smile.

Because there is only one answer.

Nobody but God.

Not my education.

Not my abilities.

Not my connections.

Not my strength.

His grace.

His mercy.

His wisdom.

His favour.

His love.

Everything good in my life points back to Him.

My Prayer for You

As you close this book, my prayer is not that you remember my name.

I pray you remember God's faithfulness.

I pray that you will believe again.

I pray that you will forgive again.

I pray that you will dream again.

I pray that you will trust again.

I pray that you will surrender every broken piece of your life to the Master Potter.

Because He specializes in restoration.

He takes shattered dreams and builds new beginnings.

He takes broken hearts and fills them with hope.

He takes financial bondage and replaces it with freedom.

He takes rejection and speaks acceptance.

He takes ordinary people and allows them to live extraordinary lives for His glory.

He did it for me.

And He can do it for **you.**

Final Life Lessons

- *Your past prepares you—it does not imprison you.*
- *Healing begins when you surrender your brokenness to God.*
- Forgiveness is freedom.
- Financial freedom starts with spiritual wisdom.
- Your testimony is one of God's greatest gifts.
- Obedience opens doors that talent alone never can.

- Success is measured by faithfulness, not possessions.
- God's timing is always perfect.
- Nothing is impossible with God.
- With God, you may be broken—but you never have to remain shattered.

Reflection Questions

1. What broken area of your life do you need to place into God's hands today?
2. Is there someone you need to forgive so you can move forward?
3. What has God already brought you through that can encourage someone else?
4. How can your testimony become part of someone else's healing?
5. What legacy do you want your life to leave for future generations?

Final Prayer

Heavenly Father,

Thank You for every chapter of my life.

Thank You for the tears that taught me to trust You.

Thank You for the disappointments that redirected me.

Thank You for the struggles that strengthened me.

Thank You for the failures that humbled me.

Thank You for the victories that reminded me You are faithful.

Lord, I surrender every remaining broken place in my heart. Continue shaping me into the woman You created me to be. Never allow success to replace humility or blessing to replace my dependence on You.

I pray for every reader holding this book. Wherever they are in life, meet them there. Heal wounded hearts, restore broken families, strengthen weary minds, provide for every need, and remind them that You have not forgotten them.

Give them courage to forgive, faith to believe, wisdom to steward what You provide, and hope to keep moving forward.

May they discover, just as I have, that no matter how painful the past has been, You are still the God who restores.

Let every page of this testimony point people to Jesus Christ, the Author and Finisher of our faith.

And when people look at my life, let them never see me first.

Let them see You.

For every blessing, every breakthrough, every healed wound, every restored relationship, every debt paid, every opportunity, every home, every business, every life changed, and every miracle can be summed up in three unforgettable words:

Nobody But God.

In the mighty and matchless name of Jesus Christ,

Amen.

Closing Declaration

I was broken...

But I was never abandoned.

I was wounded...

But I was never destroyed.

I was rejected...

But I was always chosen by God.

I faced debt...

But God taught me stewardship and freedom.

I experienced loss...

But God gave me purpose.

I carried shame...

But God clothed me with grace.

I walked through storms...

But God became my shelter.

I stand today as living proof that what God begins, He faithfully completes.

I was broken…

But by the grace of God…

I Was Never Shattered.

Author's Final Word

If you've read this far, thank you for allowing me to share my heart, my journey, and the lessons God has taught me along the way.

As I reflect on my life, I realize that many of my decisions were rooted in experiences I didn't fully understand at the time.

As a little girl, my mother taught me the importance of taking care of my outward appearance. She made sure my hair was done, my nails were manicured, and I was dressed nicely. Those were acts of love from a sixteen-year-old mother who did the very best she could with what she had. Looking back, I now understand that she was giving me what she knew how to give.

As I grew older, however, I unknowingly placed too much value on the external. I believed that if I looked successful, people would see me differently. If I dressed well, drove a nice car, wore beautiful jewelry, and lived in a nice home, perhaps I would finally feel accepted and accomplished. I learned to present an image of success long before I actually experienced it.

My relationships also shaped the way I viewed life.

After experiencing heartbreaks, disappointments, and broken trust, I made a decision that I would never allow myself to become dependent on a man for my survival. I wanted the freedom to make decisions because they were right—not because I needed someone to provide for me. I wanted to stand on my own, build my own career, earn my own income, and never feel forced to compromise my values simply to make ends meet.

There is nothing wrong with desiring success or financial independence. In fact, I believe God wants us to be wise stewards and to prosper in every area of our lives. But somewhere along the way, I confused **looking successful** with **being financially secure**.

I became exhausted from living paycheck to paycheck.

I grew weary of robbing Peter to pay Paul.

I grew tired of carrying the weight of debt, worrying about bills, wondering how I would make it to the next payday, and pretending everything was fine when it wasn't.

Financial brokenness is exhausting.

Emotional brokenness is exhausting.

Living behind a mask is exhausting.

It wasn't until I surrendered every part of my life to God—my heart, my finances, my fears, and my dreams—that true transformation began.

God changed more than my bank account.

He changed my thinking.

He changed my priorities.

He changed my definition of success.

Today, I understand that success is not measured by the car you drive, the clothes you wear, the home you live in, or the title behind your name.

Success is living in the will of God.

Success is having peace instead of pretending.

Success is being debt-free enough to be generous.

Success is having the freedom to say "yes" to God without finances standing in the way.

Every tear I cried...

Every relationship that ended...

Every rejection...

Every financial mistake...

Every sleepless night...

Every disappointment...

Every lesson...

None of it was wasted.

God used every painful experience to prepare me for my purpose.

Today, those same struggles have become the foundation of my passion for helping others break free from financial bondage, emotional brokenness, and limiting beliefs. My story is no longer about what I lost—it is about what God restored.

If sharing my journey helps even one person avoid the mistakes I made, find hope in the middle of their pain, or believe that restoration is possible, then every chapter of my life has been worth it.

I leave you with this final thought:

Your greatest pain may become your greatest purpose.

Your deepest struggle may become someone else's survival guide.

And what the enemy intended to destroy you with, God can use to deliver someone else.

Never be ashamed of your story.

It may be the very testimony God uses to change a life.

Thank you for taking this journey with me.

May you always remember...

Broken things can still be used.

You may be broken...

But by the grace of God, you never have to be shattered.

To God be all the glory.

Karen B. Turnage
Author, *Broken But Not Shattered*

Broken But Not Shattered

by Karen B. Turnage

Encouragement for the Broken Woman

- ❖ "You may be broken, but you are not shattered. God can still create something beautiful from every piece."
- ❖ "Your brokenness is not the end of your story—it may simply be the beginning of God's greatest work in your life."
- ❖ "What broke your heart does not have the authority to break your future."
- ❖ "You survived what you thought would destroy you. Now allow God to show you why He kept you."
- ❖ "Stop measuring your worth by who rejected you. God chose you before they ever had an opportunity to overlook you."
- ❖ "Some doors closed because God knew what was waiting for you on the other side."
- ❖ "You don't have to keep bleeding from wounds God is ready to heal."
- ❖ "The woman you are becoming will understand why the woman you used to be had to survive so much."

- **“You were never created to spend your life begging people to recognize the value God already placed inside of you.”**
- **“Being rejected by people does not mean you have been rejected by God.”**
- **“Sometimes God allows the pieces to fall so He can rebuild your life according to His design instead of yours.”**
- **“Your scars are evidence that the wound did not win.”**
- **“You can forgive what happened without giving it permission to continue controlling your life.”**
- **“The right relationship will never require you to lose yourself just to keep someone else.”**
- **“You are allowed to outgrow the version of yourself that learned to survive by settling.”**
- **“There comes a time when survival is no longer enough. God wants you healed, whole, free, and living abundantly.”**
- **“You don't have to look successful while suffering financially. Peace is worth more than appearances.”**

- ❖ "Financial freedom begins when you stop spending to impress people and start managing money to change your future."
- ❖ "Your past explains some of your wounds, but it does not get to determine your destiny."
- ❖ "God can take the very thing that once made you cry and turn it into the testimony that helps another woman survive."
- ❖ "The pressure didn't destroy you—it revealed the strength God had already placed inside of you."
- ❖ "Don't be ashamed of the woman who struggled. She fought hard to become the woman you are today."
- ❖ "You don't need an invitation to every table. When God has a seat for you, nobody can give it away."
- ❖ "You spent enough years asking, 'Why me?' One day you may realize the answer was, 'Because I am going to use you.
- ❖ "Broken things can still be used. God specializes in restoration."

"I thought my brokenness disqualified me. God showed me that it was preparing me. The pain became my testimony, the struggle became my strength, and the

broken pieces became my purpose."
— Karen B. Turnage

Broken But Not Shattered

by Karen B. Turnage